FOR

DUMMIES®

POCKET EDITION

by Ed McCarthy and Mary Ewing-Mulligan

WILEY

Wiley Publishing, Inc.

Italian Wine For Dummies®, Pocket Edition

Published by
Wiley Publishing, Inc.
111 River Street
Hoboken, NJ 07030-5774
www.wiley.com

Copyright © 2009 by Wiley Publishing, Inc., Indianapolis, Indiana

Published by Wiley Publishing, Inc., Indianapolis, Indiana

Published simultaneously in Canada

Contents at a Glance

Introduction

● ●

*A*t this moment in time, Italy is the most exciting wine country on earth. The quality of the wines has never been higher, and the range of wines has never been broader. Nor have more types of Italian wines ever been available outside of Italy.

The quality of Italy's wines has been growing steadily for about two decades. Now, finally, the message has leaked beyond the small cult of wine lovers who have loyally followed Italian wines, and into the mainstream of America's wine consciousness. You can now find Italian wines in three-star French restaurants. California wineries are trying their hand with Italian grape varieties and Italianate wine styles. New York City even boasts two all-Italian wine shops.

Although Italy's wines are more desirable and more available than ever, they're no more comprehensible. In fact, the proliferation of new wines and new wine zones has made Italian wine an even more confusing topic than it's always been. (All the obscure grape varieties, complicated wine blends, strange wine names, and restrictive wine laws — observed or circumvented — make Italian wines just about the most challenging of all to master.) Yet comprehensive, up-to-date reference books on Italian wines simply weren't available in English. *Italian Wine For Dummies,* Pocket Edition, begins to change all that.

Icons Used in This Book

Advice and information that makes you a wiser Italian wine drinker is marked by this bull's-eye so that you won't miss it.

When you see this sign, you know that you're in the territory of a common misunderstanding about Italy's wine. We alert you to help prevent confusion.

Some issues in wine are so fundamental that they bear repeating. Just so you don't think we repeated ourselves without realizing it, we mark the repetitions with this symbol.

Where to Go from Here

You've got your minibook copy of *Italian Wine For Dummies*, Pocket Edition — now what? This minibook is a reference, so if you want to know more about Super-Tuscans, head to Chapter 3. Or if you're interested in finding out more about Barolos, flip to Chapter 2. Or heck, start with Chapter 1 and read the chapters in order . . . you rebel. If you want even more advice about Italian wines, from the intricacies of wine laws and labels to the wines of Sicily, check out the full-size version of *Italian Wine For Dummies* — simply head to your local book seller or go to www.dummies.com.

Chapter 1
Born to Make Wine

· ·

In This Chapter

▶ A leader of the pack

▶ Forty centuries of winemaking experience

▶ Italy's wine diversity formula

▶ The trend toward quality

· ·

*W*hen most people think of Italy, they think of food. (History, art, or fast cars might be other associations — but food would have to be right up there, near the top of the list.)

As central as food is to Italy's personality, so is wine. For most Italians, wine *is* food, no less essential to every meal than bread or family. Wine, in fact, *is* family, and community, because nearly every Italian either knows someone who makes wine or makes wine himself.

Wine to Boot

The Italian peninsula, with its fan-like top and its long, boot-like body, has the most recognizable shape of any country on earth. But its recognition exceeds its actual size. Italy is a small land; the whole country is less than three-quarters the size of California.

4

Despite its small size, Italy's role in the world of wine is huge:

- ✔ Italy produces more wine than any other country on earth, in many years. (When Italy isn't the world's number one wine producer, it's number two, behind France.) Italy's annual wine production is generally about 1.5 billion gallons, the equivalent of more than 8 billion bottles! Nearly 30 percent of all the world's wine comes from Italy.

- ✔ Italy has more vineyard land than any other country except Spain. Vines grow in every nook and cranny of the peninsula and the islands.

- ✔ Italy boasts dozens of native grape varieties, many of which are successful only in Italy.

- ✔ Italy produces hundreds of wines — nearly 1,000 different types, we'd say.

Although the land called Italy has a long, proud history, the country became a unified nation only in 1861, and has existed in its present form only since 1919, when the Austro-Hungarian Empire ceded certain northern territories to Italy after World War I. Politically, Italy today consists of 20 regions, similar to states — 18 on the mainland and two islands; these 20 political regions are also Italy's wine regions. (Figure 1-1 shows Italy's 20 regions.) Because of the country's relative youth, diverse cultures exist in different parts of the country, and regional pride runs stronger than national pride. Italy's wines reflect these diverse cultures.

Figure 1-1: Italy's 20 wine regions.

From the Alps to almost Africa

When we think about Italy's shape, location, and topography, we have to chuckle at the improbability of it all. Italy starts in the Alps but ends fairly close to Africa; it has a long, long seacoast but very little flat land; it has three major mountain ranges dividing it from other countries and segregating its regions from one another. Italy has everything, all together, in a small package of disjointed pieces that's isolated from everything around it.

The mountain ranges are the Alps in the northwest, separating Italy from Switzerland and France; the Dolomites, actually part of the Alps, separating north-eastern Italy from Austria; and the Apennines, starting in the northwest and running like a spine down the Italian boot, separating the regions of the east coast from those of the west.

Italy's major expanse of flat land is the Po River Valley, which begins in western Piedmont and extends east-ward until the Po empties into the Adriatic Sea just north of Emilia-Romagna's border with the Veneto (see Figure 1-1). Most of Italy's rice, grain, maize, and fruit crops come from this area; the rest of the country grows olive trees, garden vegetables, and, of course, grapes. In most of Italy, you can't travel five miles with-out seeing vines.

Wine from Day One

Grape growing is an historic occupation in Italy. When Phoenician traders arrived in Puglia 4,000 years ago, wine already existed there. The Etruscans grew wine grapes in Central Italy from the 8th to the 4th century B.C. By the 3rd century B.C., grapes grew in much of today's Italy, and the Romans get credit for dispersing the vine throughout western Europe.

Diverse conditions, diverse wines

What makes Italy an ideal and unique territory for growing grapes is precisely its improbable combination of natural conditions:

- ✔ The range of latitudes creates a wide variety of climatic conditions from north to south.

- ✔ The foothills of the mountains provide slopes ideal for vineyards, as well as higher altitudes for cool climate grape growing.

- ✔ The varied terrain — seacoast, hills, and mountains — within many regions provides a diversity of growing conditions even within single regions.

- ✔ The segregated nature of the regions has enabled local grape varieties to survive in near isolation.

When it comes to wine production, Italy's odd situation is a formula for variety (and a formula for confusion on the part of those trying to master Italian wines!). Different grape varieties make different wines in different regions. And the same grape variety makes different wines in different parts of a single region. In a nutshell, that's why Italy makes so many different wines.

Italian Wine Styles Today

Wine is so universally accepted within Italy, and so ubiquitous, that most Italians traditionally took it for granted. This casual attitude has changed somewhat in recent years, but it has taken its toll: Although Italy has some great, great wines, these wines haven't enjoyed nearly the prestige of France's top wines. (That situation is only now beginning to change.) And, considering how many wines Italy makes, only a small percentage are widely available in U.S. wine shops. The silver lining is that some of Italy's wines are still fairly inexpensive.

Italian wine producers today are more serious about their wine than they have ever been, and the quality of Italian wine is at an all-time high. (Recent excellent vintages have only helped.) As producers experiment with new techniques in their vineyards and wineries, new styles of Italian wine are emerging, and the traditional styles are improving. As a result, Italian wines today are more varied than ever. Congratulations on choosing a great time to discover Italian wine!

The Italian prototype

The fundamental style of Italian wine derives from the fact that Italians view wine as a mealtime beverage; a wine's first responsibility is to go well with food. The prototypical Italian red or white wine has the following characteristics:

- ✔ High acidity, which translates as crispness in the whites and firmness in the reds (high-acid wines are very food-friendly)
- ✔ No sweetness
- ✔ Fairly subdued, subtle aromas and flavors (so as not to compete with food)
- ✔ Light to medium body (although many full-bodied wines do exist)

If you imagine such a wine, you can understand that it's a wine without illusions of grandeur, a straightforward beverage that might not win a wine competition but is a welcome dinner companion.

Variations on the prototype in recent years have included some of the following characteristics:

- ✔ More concentrated flavor and slightly fuller body, due to greater ripeness in the grapes (thanks to improved vineyard practices)

- ✔ Smoky or toasty aromas and flavors from small oak barrels

- ✔ Fruitier aromas and flavors — although the wines are still much less fruity than, say, the typical Californian or Australian wine

Red, white, and beyond

About two-thirds of all Italian wine is red. Every region makes red wine, even the cool northern regions and especially the South. But Italy makes plenty of white, too — particularly Northeast and Central Italy. Rosé wine is only a minor category.

Italy's production of sparkling wine is considerable, especially in the North. Italian sparkling wines include sweet styles, such as Asti, and fully dry styles. Dessert wines are a serious specialty of some regions. These sweet wines include wines from grapes dried after the harvest (to concentrate their sugar); wines from late-harvested grapes affected with "noble rot" (*Wine For Dummies,* 4th Edition, by us, published by Wiley, explains noble rot); and wines that are fortified with alcohol to preserve their natural sweetness.

A Note about Names

If you can show that your climate, soil, or other natural condition (including human factors, such as tradition) is different from that of a nearby area, then you presumably make a different type of wine than that other area — and, upon request, the authorities can give you a unique, official name for your type of wine.

Italy's official wine names are called DOC or DOCG names:

- ✔ DOC stands for *Denominazione di Origine Controllata* (dae-no-mee-naht-zee-*oh*-nae-dee-oh-*ree*-gee-nae-con-trol-*lah*-tah), which translates as "controlled (or protected) place name"; the long Italian phrase appears on the wine label.

- ✔ DOCG stands for *Denominazione di Origine Controllata e Garantita* (. . . ae-gah-rahn-*tee*-tah), which translates as "controlled and guaranteed place name"; this even longer Italian phrase appears on the labels of DOCG wines.

Every DOC or DOCG wine comes from a specific place that's defined by law, is made from specific grapes stipulated by the law (although sometimes the law gives producers a lot of leeway in their choice of grapes), is aged for a certain length of time, and so forth. In the end, a wine that carries a DOC or DOCG name should taste more or less the way the law says that wine should taste, although the official taste descriptions are loose; for example, they might say that a particular wine should taste "dry, crisp, harmonious, and slightly tannic." Lots of room for interpretation there.

Chapter 2
The Wines of Piedmont

* *

In This Chapter
▶ Two red superstars
▶ The re-birth of Barbera
▶ Asti, a world-class sparkler
▶ Nebbiolo, north and south

* *

Piedmont, Italy's northwestern-most region, is remote from the rest of mainland Italy. The remoteness of this part of Italy has helped to preserve local traditions, local cuisine, and local wine styles. And we're not just talking about quaint local color: Some of the wines from northwestern Italy are among Italy's very greatest, period.

The Majesty of Piedmont

True to its name, Piedmont — "foot of the mountain" — is surrounded by mountains on three sides. The mighty Alps separate it from France to the west and from Switzerland (and the tiny Aosta Valley region) to the north, while the Apennines separate it from the region of Liguria to the south (see Figure 1-1). Most of Piedmont's best wines come either from the foothills of the Apennines in the south or the foothills of the Alps in the north.

Piedmont generally has a continental climate: cold winters and mainly dry, hot summers. The mild autumns, with heavy fog especially in southern Piedmont, are extremely beneficial for late-ripening grape varieties, such as Nebbiolo — Piedmont's finest variety.

The wines of Piedmont

Piedmont — specifically the Barolo and Barbaresco districts — was the first region in Italy to recognize the importance of making separate wines from exceptional vineyards, a concept that Burgundy and other regions of France had practiced for some time. Producers such as Vietti and Prunotto began making single-vineyard Barolos and Barbarescos in 1961.

About 90 percent of Piedmont's wine comes from the southern part of the region. This production roughly falls into the following two areas:

- The Alba area, in southcentral Piedmont, which includes the Langhe Hills area and the Roero area
- The Asti/Alessandria area, in southeast Piedmont, extending south of the Po River to the border with Liguria, and including the Monferrato Hills

Additionally, wine comes from two separate parts of northern Piedmont, and from a few, scattered wine zones in the pre-Alpine, western part of the region.

The grapes of Piedmont

Piedmont boasts three major red grape varieties and two major white varieties. These varieties are the following:

- **Nebbiolo:** A noble but difficult, late-ripening red variety that nowhere in the world grows as well and makes such superb wine (when conditions are right) as it does in the Langhe (*lahn*-gae) hills around the town of Alba.

- ✔ **Barbera:** A native red Piedmontese variety that until a few decades ago was Italy's most planted red variety; in Piedmont it grows mainly in the Asti and Alba areas, making serious as well as everyday wines.

- ✔ **Dolcetto:** A spicy red variety seldom seen outside Piedmont; it's widely grown in the Alba and southeastern areas of the region.

- ✔ **Moscato:** A world-renowned white grape with floral aromas and flavors; a specialty of the Asti area.

- ✔ **Cortese:** A grape that makes delicately-flavored dry white wines; a specialty of the Gavi area.

Wines of the Alba Area

The Alba wine zone consists of two areas in southcentral Piedmont, the Langhe hills and the Roero, which surround the town of Alba. This fairly small area produces Northern Italy's two greatest red wines — Barolo and Barbaresco — as well as several others of note.

Barolo

A well-made Barolo from a good vintage is one of the greatest red wines in the world. It's powerful and full-bodied, with all sorts of intriguing aromas and flavors — ripe strawberries, tar, mint and/or eucalyptus, licorice, camphor, tobacco, chocolate, roses, spices, vanilla, and white truffles — and it only gets better with age. Often referred to as "the king of wines," Barolo is austere and tannic in its youth, and it usually requires many years of aging before it is ready to drink — and even then, decanting and aerating the wine help soften it. Barolo's longevity is foreshadowed by its production regulations: The wine must age a minimum of three years before release (five for *riservas*). Along with Italy's other two big "B" wines — Barbaresco and Brunello di Montalcino — Barolo was among the first Italian wines granted DOCG status in 1980.

Barolo must be made entirely from the Nebbiolo grape. This is its blessing and its curse. The Nebbiolo variety expresses itself brilliantly in the Barolo and Barbaresco zones of the Langhe hills. The marly clay soil is alkaline enough to tame the fiercely high acidity of Nebbiolo. In most years, there's enough warmth from the sun and just enough rain; most importantly, the mild, foggy autumns provide enough time for the notoriously late-ripening Nebbiolo to slowly complete its growth. (The grape's name probably comes from the Italian word for "fog," *nebbia*.) The curse of Nebbiolo is that weather conditions don't always allow it to ripen sufficiently — in which case Nebbiolo's tannin and acidity can be too great, making harsh wine.

The intricacies of a tiny DOCG zone

Basically, five communities produce most (87 percent) of Barolo, and most of the best Barolo:

- ✔ La Morra
- ✔ Barolo
- ✔ Serralunga d'Alba
- ✔ Castiglione Falletto
- ✔ Monforte d'Alba

Not counting the producers' individual imprints, two different types of Barolo exist, according to the location of the vineyards:

- ✔ The Barolo wines of the Serralunga (eastern) Valley — which includes the communities of Serralunga d'Alba, Castiglione Falletto, and Monforte d'Alba — tend to be more austere, powerful, and long-lived; they are more tannic and more full-bodied than other Barolos, generally have more extract (solid grape matter) and alcohol, and require long aging — 12 to 15 years — to develop and mature.

- ✔ The Barolo wines of the Central (western) Valley — basically the largest community, La Morra, which accounts for about one-third of all Barolo wine, and part of the community of Barolo — often have more perfumed aromas, such as white truffles; they are typically more elegant and have a velvety texture, are less full-bodied, and are less tannic than the Barolos of the Serralunga Valley. They are usually ready to drink sooner — often within eight to ten years of their vintage date.

Vineyards in the commune of Barolo itself, which extend into both valleys, make both styles of Barolo wine — depending on their location and, to some extent, the wine producer.

Recommended Barolo producers

We list our very favorite Barolo producers alphabetically, and the communes where most, or all, of their vineyards are located.

Giacomo Conterno (Serralunga d'Alba)

Gaja (Serralunga d'Alba; La Morra)

Bruno Giacosa (Serralunga d'Alba; Castiglione Falletto)

Bartolo Mascarello (Barolo)

Giuseppe Mascarello (Castiglione Falletto; Monforte d'Alba)

Giuseppe Rinaldi (Barolo; La Morra)

Luciano Sandrone (Barolo)

Paolo Scavino (Castiglione Falletto)

Vietti (Castiglione Falletto)

Barbaresco

The other great red wine of the Langhe hills, Barbaresco (bahr-bah-*res*-co), also a DOCG wine, is very similar to Barolo. Both Barolo and Barbaresco are made entirely from Nebbiolo, share similar soils and climate (because they are within ten miles of each other), and many producers make both wines, using similar production methods.

Barbaresco is a sturdy, austere, powerful wine, generally only slightly less full-bodied than Barolo: Its minimum alcohol content is slightly less (12.5 percent, compared to 13 percent for Barolo), and its minimum aging at the winery (two years minimum, four for *riservas*) is one year less than Barolo's.

The aromas and flavors of Barbaresco wines are very much the same as those of Barolo. But Barbaresco is more elegant, typically less austere, and more accessible in its youth. For this reason, it is generally a better choice in restaurants, especially when most of the available wines are from recent vintages.

Because Barbaresco has fewer producers than Barolo, in a smaller, more consistent territory, it's a more consistently reliable wine, generally speaking. About 200 producers make Barolo, quite a few of whom are not very good. On the other hand, we seldom come across a poor Barbaresco producer.

Vineyard and winemaking styles in the Barbaresco zone

The soils of the vineyards around the three villages where the grapes for Barbaresco grow are more uniform than those of the Barolo communities; consequently, you don't see such striking differences among Barbaresco wines as you do among Barolos. But some differences do exist among Barbarescos according to their vineyard area (remember that winemaking style can camouflage the characteristics of the vineyard area, however):

- ✔ The community of Neive, on the next hill east of Barbaresco, produces the most full-bodied, tannic Barbarescos in the region. Neive accounts for almost 31 percent of Barbaresco and is the home of the great Bruno Giacosa, as well as Fratelli Cigliuti and the historic Castello di Neive.

- ✔ The wines of the Barbaresco community tend to be a bit lighter in color and lighter-bodied than those of Neive, but they are known for their perfumed aromas and their structure.

- ✔ Treiso d'Alba (or simply, Treiso), south of Barbaresco, is the least-known of the three areas; its Barbarescos tend to be lighter-bodied than the others, and they are known for their finesse and their elegance.

Recommended Barbaresco producers

We list our favorite Barbaresco producers alphabetically, and name the communes where most, or all, of
their vineyards are located. Many Barolo producers
also make good Barbarescos.

Ceretto, also known as
Bricco Asili (Barbaresco)

Fratelli Cigliuti (Neive)

Angelo Gaja (Barbaresco)

Bruno Giacosa (Neive)

Marchesi di Gresy
(Barbaresco)

Roagna, also know as I
Paglieri (Barbaresco)

Albino Rocca (Barbaresco)

Bruno Rocca (Barbaresco)

La Spinetta (Neive)

La Spinona (Barbaresco)

Barbera, Dolcetto, and Nebbiolo of Alba

The town of Alba gives its name to three red varietal
wines, each made entirely from its named grape:
Barbera d'Alba (bar-*bae*-rah-*dahl*-bah), Dolcetto d'Alba
(dohl-*chet*-toh-*dahl*-bah), and Nebbiolo d'Alba (nehb-
bee-*oh*-loh-*dahl*-bah).

Barbera

Of these three, Barbera d'Alba is generally the finest
and most serious wine. Barbera is a strange variety. It
has lots of pigmentation and very high acidity, but
almost no tannin in its skins and seeds. Its wines are
therefore dark in color but crisp and refreshing, rather
like white wines, instead of being firm and mouth-
drying like most reds — but its berry-cherry and spicy
flavors are red wine all the way.

Barbera d'Alba is enjoyable both young and with age, up to about 15 years, to our taste — although as it ages beyond about eight years, it loses its spicy vibrancy and becomes a more normalized red wine. Simple, inexpensive Barbera is our favorite wine with pizza, but the best examples are really too good for such casual food. Barbera is terrific with pasta with tomato sauce, spicy foods, bitter greens, and hearty dishes.

Our favorite producers of Barbera d'Alba, listed alphabetically, are the following:

Elio Altare	Bartolo Mascarello
Elvio Cogno	Giuseppe Mascarello
Aldo Conterno	Moccagatta
Giacomo Conterno	Prunotto
Gaja	Giuseppi Rinaldi
Manzone	Paolo Scavino
Marcarini	Vietti

Dolcetto d'Alba

Dolcetto d'Alba comes from vineyards in the Langhe hills and is made entirely from Dolcetto, which ripens earlier than other red varieties of the area. Dolcetto d'Alba is also earlier maturing as a wine than Barbera or Nebbiolo, and in meals is usually served before Barbera — to accompany the five or six (or eight) antipasto courses of a typical Piedmontese meal.

Dolcetto has lower acidity than Barbera, but it's still acidic, as any self-respecting Italian wine should be; its acid suits it well to food. It's more tannic than

Barbera — a dry, medium-bodied, rich-textured wine with aromas and flavors of black pepper and ripe berry fruit.

 We love to drink Dolcetto with some of the same kind of foods as Barbera — pizza, somewhat spicy dishes, earthy vegetarian foods — but it's also terrific with casual meals such as chef salads, cold cuts, sandwiches, or turkey burgers. Dolcetto d'Alba costs about $12 to $20 per bottle, and is best when it's no more than three years old, in our opinion. Many Barolo producers also make Dolcetto d'Alba; our favorite producers, alphabetically, are Elio Altare, Clerico, Elvio Cogno (a specialty), Giacomo Conterno, Conterno-Fantino, Marcarini, Ratti, Sandrone, and Vietti.

Nebbiolo d'Alba

To our way of thinking, Nebbiolo d'Alba runs a distant third among the three Alba varietal wines. Not that it's not a perfectly fine, well-made wine most of the time; we just prefer to experience Nebbiolo in its most dramatic, highest-quality expression — as Barolo and Barbaresco. Nebbiolo d'Alba lacks the intensity and flair of those wines, and instead is just a good, medium-bodied, firm red wine with delicate flavors of tar, red fruits, and herbs.

Nebbiolo d'Alba is a relatively light style of Nebbiolo for drinking young; the wine must age only one year before release. Its best drinkability period is three to seven years from the vintage, in our opinion. Also to its advantage, it's relatively inexpensive — generally about $15 to $18 a bottle. One Barolo producer who makes a specialty of producing fine Nebbiolo d'Alba is Tenuta Carretta.

The Wines of Asti and Alessandria

East and north of the Alba area are the provinces of Asti and Alessandria This is the area of the Monferrato Hills, which extend from the Po River south to the Apennines. The name Monferrato appears as part of many wine names, as does Asti, the province — but oddly enough, not Alessandria.

Nebbiolo recedes in importance in Asti and Alessandria, and Barbera comes strongly to the foreground — along with a minor red variety called Grignolino (gree-n'yoh-*lee*-no), the red Malvasia, the white Cortese (cor-*tae*-sae) grape, and, above all, Moscato.

Asti is a famous name around the world, even to those who have never visited that city. The reason is the DOCG wine called Asti, Italy's flagship sparkling wine and one of the most unique sparkling wines in the world. Asti is made entirely from the Moscato grape — the Muscat à Petits Grains type, the best Muscat variety of all. It's a sweet, absolutely delicious bubbly with rich floral, peachy flavors and lots of acidity to balance its sweetness.

Asti is all about freshness. Once the wine is about two or three years old, it starts to taste richer and somewhat heavy — still tasty, but no longer at its best. To complicate the matter, however, Asti doesn't carry a vintage date, so you don't know *how* old a particular bottle really is. Our suggestion is to purchase Asti from a store that sells a lot of it, and to purchase a brand that sells well, because the

turnover assures freshness. Our favorite
brands are Fontanafredda, Martini & Rossi,
and Cinzano, but freshness is even more
important than which brand you choose. And
make sure the wine is genuine Asti; imitations
do exist!

A companion wine to Asti — made from the same
grapes in the same vineyard areas and covered under
the same DOCG — is Moscato d'Asti (mo-*scah*-toh-*dahs*-
tee). This wine is quite similar to Asti except that it's
just *frizzante* — lightly bubbly, or fizzy — rather than
sparkling, and its flavors are more delicate than Asti's.
It's also even lower in alcohol — generally from 5 to 7.5
percent (in some states, that's technically too low to be
wine!). Freshness is even more crucial for Moscato
d'Asti than it is for Asti, but fortunately the wines are
vintage dated. Buy the youngest vintage possible, and
never buy any vintage that's more than two years old.

Our favorite Moscato d'Asti is Cascinetta,
made by Vietti; La Spinetta is a well-regarded
brand, but the wine is slightly less delicate.
Other good brands are Ceretto's Santo
Stefano, Piero Gatti, Dante Rivetti, and Paolo
Saracco.

Chapter 3
The Wines of Tuscany

*1*f you've been to Tuscany, your pulse might be racing now, as you recall the magic and wonder of the region. Whether you've experienced Tuscany first-hand or not, though, we hope that our enthusiasm for the wines of Tuscany will infect you, and that the wines will bring you as much pleasure as they bring us.

The Big Picture of Tuscany

Italy's most recent wine renaissance began in Tuscany in the early 1970s, when producers of Chianti decided to show the world once and for all that Tuscan wines deserve to be taken seriously; their quality movement changed the face of wine all over Italy.

Tuscany sits on Italy's western coast and is quite hilly (see Figure 1-1). The altitude of the hills tempers the summer heat, which can otherwise be sweltering.

Although Tuscany has plenty of vineyard land, its hillside vineyards and poor soils are geared toward quality rather than quantity of production.

About 50 percent of Tuscany's wine production is DOC or DOCG. Tuscany has six DOCG wines and 29 DOCs (depending on how you count them); the vast majority (80 percent) of this classified-level production is red wine. The six DOCG wines are the following:

- ✔ **Chianti** (key-*ahn*-tee)
- ✔ **Chianti Classico**
- ✔ **Brunello di Montalcino** (brew-*nel*-lo-dee-mahn-tahl-*chee*-no)
- ✔ **Carmignano Rosso** (car-mee-*nyah*-no)
- ✔ **Vino Nobile di Montepulciano** (*vee*-no-*no*-bee-lae-dee-mahn-tae-pool-chee-*ah*-no)
- ✔ **Vernaccia di San Gimignano** (ver-*nahch*-cha-dee-san-gee-mee-*nyah*-no)

Of these wines, only Vernaccia di San Gimignano is white.

Sangiovese is the main red grape variety of Tuscany, not just quantitatively but also qualitatively speaking. Many clones of Sangiovese exist; besides broad families of Sangiovese, such as the top-quality Sangiovese Grosso and the ordinary Sangiovese di Romagna, numerous local clones have evolved in each of the districts where the grape has traditionally grown, in response to local conditions. Sangiovese's many mutations explain why it has several different names or nicknames in Tuscany, such as Brunello, Prugnolo Gentile, and Morellino.

The next most important red variety in quality terms is Cabernet Sauvignon; this variety has grown in the region for at least 250 years, but has become especially popular since the late 1970s. Numerous other red varieties exist, including native varieties such as Mammolo, Canaiolo (cahn-eye-*oh*-lo), Malvasia Nera, and Colorino, and international varieties such as Merlot (like Cabernet, increasingly popular with growers), Pinot Noir, and Syrah.

Trebbiano is the leading white variety of the region in terms of acreage planted — and the main reason that Tuscan white wines are far less exciting than the reds. But Vermentino, a characterful and increasingly popular variety, is common in Tuscany's coastal areas, in blends and alone. The highest quality white wines derive from the Vernaccia grape, grown around San Gimignano, and from international varieties such as Chardonnay, which has grown in Tuscany for about 150 years, but has been particularly fashionable in the last two decades.

The Land of Chianti

Chianti is not just Tuscany's most famous wine — it's Italy's most famous wine, and one of the most famous wines in the entire world. But Chianti is not just one type of wine. The name embodies wines from several sub-zones, which vary quite a lot in richness and quality; it also covers wines for drinking young, and age-worthy wines; inexpensive ($8 a bottle) wines and pricey ($60) wines. What these wines have in common is that they're all red, and they're all based on the Sangiovese grape.

Will the real Chianti please stand up?

The land of Chianti has an ancient winemaking legacy. Grape growing and winemaking have existed there since the 8th century B.C. (two centuries before winemaking came to Southern France). The name "Chianti" applied to wine as early as 1398 — although in those early days, "Chianti" was also a white wine — and several wine producers who exist today can trace their companies' lineage back to the 14th century.

In 1716, the Grand Duke of Tuscany declared Chianti a wine of protected origin. But what actually was and wasn't the territory of Chianti remained a contentious subject among producers until the early 20th century. Some wanted to restrict the use of the name Chianti to a fairly small area known as Chianti in the early 15th century, while others wanted the right to use the famous name for their own wines from outlying areas. Factions formed, all of them using "Chianti" as part of their name. In 1932, a governmental decree finally put the matter to rest by recognizing all of the so-called Chianti zones as Chianti, but distinguishing the various areas with specific sub-zone names, such as Chianti Classico, Chianti Colli Fiorentini, and so forth.

Chianti Classico

Chianti Classico is not only the heartland of Tuscany — the original Chianti area, situated at the very center of Tuscany — but it is also the emotional heart of the region. The zone is populated by serious and skilled winemakers who care deeply about their land and their wines, and who infect wine lovers all over the world with their passion.

Chianti Classico encompasses four communes, or communities, in their entirety — Greve, Radda, Gaiole, and Castellina — as well as portions of five others. More than 700 grape growers farm the 24,700 acres of vineyards in this area.

Although this is not a tremendously large area, the Chianti Classico zone is quite varied in soil and climate because of altitude differences (vineyards are generally from 820 to nearly 2,000 feet high) and varying distance from the Arno River, which flows through Florence. The soil in the southern part of the area is stony and hard in some parts, clayey in others, while soil in the north, closer to Florence, is richer. Higher elevations are cooler. The southernmost part, Castelnuovo Berardegna, is warmer than most of the other parts of the zone. This diversity of climate and soil — together with the flexibility regarding grape varieties that the DOCG regulation provides, and varying winemaking styles — creates a stunning array of wines.

As generalizations go, most Chianti Classico wines are medium-bodied rather than full-bodied, firm rather than soft, with a medium amount of dry tannin, and medium to high acidity. Tart cherry or ripe cherry are the main aroma/flavor descriptors, sometimes with delicate floral or nutty notes. One characteristic of Chianti that strikes us is that the wines are fairly inexpressive in the front of your mouth; all their action happens in the middle and rear. They're completely different from most New World reds, whose richness is evident as soon as you put them in your mouth.

For several years now, we've tried to peg the styles of Chianti Classico wines to the specific commune where the grapes grow. Our experimentation has had some limited success: We've come to expect wines from Castelnuovo Berardegna to be richer and riper, Gaiole wines to be firm and structured, Panzano (part of Greve) wines to be well-concentrated, and Castellina wines (our favorite style) to have finely-tuned aromas and flavors.

The average quality level of Chianti Classico wines is quite high, and we therefore admire the wines of many dozens of producers. Here are a few of our favorites and the name of the commune where they are located is listed for each.

Barone Ricasoli, formerly Castello di Brolio (Gaiole)

Castellare di Castellina (Castellina)

Castello dei Rampolla (Panzano)

Castello di Ama (Gaiole)

Castello di Fonterutoli (Castellina)

Castello di Volpaia (Radda)

Fattoria di Felsina (Castelnuovo Berardegna)

Fontodi (Panzano)

Isole e Olena (Barberino Val d'Elsa)

Marchesi Antinori (San Casciano Val di Pesa)

La Massa (Panzano)

Monsanto (Barberino Val d'Elsa)

Podere Il Palazzino (Gaiole)

Ruffino (various estates)

San Giusto a Rentennano (Gaiole)

Chianti

The Chianti DOCG designation applies to all Chianti wines other than those made from grapes grown in the Chianti Classico area. This appellation covers wines from six specific sub-zones, as well as wines from peripheral areas. Wines from individual sub-zones may carry the name of that sub-zone on their labels, while wines from the other areas, or wines combining grapes from more than one sub-zone, simply carry the appellation Chianti DOCG.

The best Chianti wines are those from specific sub-zones; these sub-zones are the following:

- ✔ **Chianti Colli Pisane** (*coh*-lee-pee-*sah*-nae): The westernmost area, in the province of Pisa

- ✔ **Chianti Colli Fiorentini** (fee-or-en-*tee*-nee): Literally, "Florentine hills," north of Chianti Classico, in the province of Florence

- ✔ **Chianti Colli Senesi** (seh-*nae*-see): The Siena hills, the southernmost part

- ✔ **Chianti Colli Aretini** (ah-rae-*tee*-nee): The Arezzo hills, in the eastern part of the zone

- ✔ **Chianti Montalbano** (mon-tahl-*bah*-no): The northwest part of the zone

- ✔ **Chianti Rufina** (*roo*-fee-nah): The northeastern part of the zone

Of these areas, the Rufina zone probably ranks highest for the quality of its wines — and is also the one area whose wines are generally available in the U.S. (It's also the area whose name most confuses wine drinkers; Rufina [*roo*-fee-nah], the zone, has nothing to do with

Ruffino [roof-*fee*-no], the wine producer.) The Rufina area is slightly more mountainous, and less gently-hilly, than the *classico* zone. Its microclimate is cooler at night than that of the *classico* zone, and the grapes ripen more slowly because of this day-night temperature variation. Traditionally, most Chianti Rufina was relatively light-bodied and made to be enjoyed young, but since the mid-1980s, producers have also made richer, more serious and more ageworthy wines. Some Rufina wines, such as the best of Selvapiana and Frescobaldi, are among the finest of all Chiantis.

Because Chianti Classico truly dominates the export market for all types of Chianti, our list of recommended producers of Chianti DOCG is short. We list these producers alphabetically, with their sub-zone:

Fattoria di Basciano (Rufina)	Chigi Saracini (Colli Senesi)
Tenuta di Capezzana (Montalbano)	Fattoria Selvapiana (Rufina)
Castello di Farnatella (Colli Senesi)	Fattoria di Manzano (Colli Aretini)
Marchesi de' Frescobaldi (Rufina)	Fattoria di Petrolo (Colli Aretini)

Vernaccia di San Gimignano

The vineyards of San Gimignano (sahn-gee-me-*n'yah*-no) lie within the Chianti Colli Senesi area, but the local pride is the DOCG white wine, Vernaccia (ver-*nahtch*-chah).

Vernaccia di San Gimignano is Tuscany's finest type of white wine — and has been, for seven centuries. It derives at least 90 percent from the Vernaccia grape variety, which is famous only here. Generally, Vernaccia is a fairly full-bodied, dry, soft white, with honey, mineral, and earthy flavors, but it sometimes is quite fruity.

 The wine varies quite a lot in style according to its winemaking: Some producers ferment or age the wine in small French oak barrels, which gives the wine a toastiness or a creaminess that it doesn't otherwise have, while other producers make the wine un-oaked, so that the mineral aromas and flavors shine through more clearly. Some producers make more than one Vernaccia wine, each a different style.

We recommend the following producers of Vernaccia di San Gimignano, listed alphabetically:

Baroncini

Vincenzo Cesani

Fattoria di Cusona

Casale-Falchini

La Lastra

Montenidoli

Mormoraia

Palagetto

Giovanni Panizzi

Fattoria Il Paradiso

Fattoria San Quirico

Teruzzi & Puthod

Fratelli Vagnoni

Monumental Montalcino

In terms of international renown, the Montalcino (mon-tal-*chee*-no) area is Tuscany's second most important wine zone, after Chianti Classico. In terms of quality, however, it's Tuscany's star.

The Montalcino wine district is a hilly, densely wooded area surrounding the town, which sits slightly northeast of the district's geographic center. The particular climate, soils, altitudes, and hillside aspects of the vineyards combine to create a singular effect: that Montalcino is the finest location on earth for the Sangiovese grape.

Montalcino's signature wine is Brunello (brew-*nel*-lo) di Montalcino, a hefty red wine made entirely from Sangiovese. (Brunello is the local, but unofficial, name for Sangiovese.) In the isolated hills of Montalcino, Sangiovese ripens better than elsewhere in Tuscany, giving wines with more color, body, extract, tannin, and richness than other wines based on the same variety.

Not that other Sangiovese wines are necessarily based on exactly the same grapes, however: The various clones of Sangiovese that grow in Montalcino are believed to be distinct from those elsewhere in Tuscany, because they evolved in response to the conditions of Montalcino. In the mid 1800s, a local named Clemente Santi isolated the clones most suited to making a high-quality, ageworthy, 100-percent Sangiovese wine, in an age when easy-to-drink, blended wines were the norm in Montalcino, as in Chianti. The wines of his grandson, Ferruccio Biondi-Santi, and a handful of other producers became celebrated during the second half of the 19th century, and affirmed the special synergy that Brunello and Montalcino share.

Today, about 200 grape growers — mostly small farmers — exist in Montalcino, and Brunello di Montalcino is considered one of Italy's two best wines. It was the first wine to earn DOCG status, in 1980, and it is generally among Italy's most expensive wines. But production is small: Only about 333,000 cases of Brunello di Montalcino are made each year.

Aging and ageability

Since its earliest conception, Brunello di Montalcino has been a wine for aging. Some wines from good vintages not only can age for 50 years or more, but in fact *need* a couple of decades to lose the fire of youth and become harmonious. The DOCG regulations echo the wine's potential by requiring that Brunello age for four years before it can be released — the longest minimum aging period for any wine in Italy; Brunello di Montalcino Riserva, made from a producer's best wines in very good vintages, must age five years before release. For at least two of these four or five years, the wine must age in oak barrels or casks.

Traditional-minded producers age their wine for three years or more in large, old casks, producing more austere wines, while the most avant-garde producers age some of their Brunello in small barrels of French oak (and practice other non-traditional winemaking techniques) to fix a certain fruitiness in their wine. In either case, almost every Brunello is best with *at least* ten years of age from the vintage.

Recommended Brunello producers

Here we name our favorite producers of Brunello di Montalcino. We list them alphabetically:

Altesino

Castello Banfi

Biondi-Santi (expensive)

Canalicchio di Sopra

Case Basse of Soldera (very expensive)

Castelgiocondo

Ciacci Piccolomini

Costanti   Poggio Antico

Il Greppone Mazzi   Il Poggione

Pertimali di Livio Sassetti   La Torre

The "Noble Wine" of Montepulciano

The second red Tuscan wine to attain DOCG status in 1980, Vino Nobile di Montepulciano (*vee*-no-*no*-bee-lae-dee-mahn-tae-pul-chee-*ah*-no), has a proud history dating back to the 17th century, when the local wine of the Montepulciano territory was dubbed "noble" because it was a favorite of noblemen. In more recent times, the producers of the Montepulciano zone have worked hard to maintain an elite image for their wine, in the face of stiff competition from both Chianti Classico and Brunello di Montalcino. But Vino Nobile's day might finally have come (again): The Montepulciano zone now seems to have attained a "critical mass" of serious producers, and the wines today are finer than we remember their being in the last 30 years.

Just like Chianti Classico, Vino Nobile di Montepulciano has reinvented itself since the mid-1980s. The wine has changed from a multi-faceted blend (of Sangiovese, Canaiolo, Mammolo, other red varieties, and white varieties) to a straightforward red wine based largely on Sangiovese. Renovation of some of the vineyards has resulted in riper grapes that make a darker, richer wine. And changes within the wineries — notably the use of French oak barrels — have further beefed up the wines' intensity. The regulation requiring the wine to age for two years in oak (or three years, for the *riserva* version) has come under review, with an eye to shortening the aging time. "Foreign" investment, from Swiss owners as well as famous Chianti houses such as Antinori and Ruffino, has also given the zone new impetus — as has the recent, exceptional 1997 vintage.

Vino Nobile is still in transition. Some wines today are soft, rich wines with creamy, plummy fruit flavors and toasty oak notes, while others are relatively lean but smooth with firm tannin and gentle almondy and red fruit flavors. In general, they range in price from about $18 to $30, with some single-vineyard wines costing slightly more.

We list here our favorite producers of Vino Nobile di Montepulciano alphabetically:

Avignonesi	Fassati
Poderi Boscarelli	Lodola Nuova
La Braccesca	Poliziano
Fattoria del Cerro	Tenuta Trerose
Dei	

Super-Tuscan Wines — The Winds of Change

The category of so-called Super-Tuscan wines is a mixed bag of wines from all over Tuscany, mainly red but also white. It's a completely unofficial category; in fact, according to how wines are normally classified in Italy, the category of Super-Tuscans doesn't even exist.

But for 20 years now, wine lovers and wine profession-
als have used the term to refer to certain wines from
Tuscany.

What are these wines? They are expensive wines ($45
and up) of small production, usually internationally-
styled (with fairly pronounced fruitiness and lots of
oakiness), usually made from grape varieties or blends
that aren't traditional in Tuscany, and carrying fanciful
names.

To grasp exactly what Super-Tuscan wines are, con-
sider their origins. Thirty years ago, Chianti had to contain at least 10 percent of white varieties in its blend,
and Sangiovese could be no more than 70 percent of
the wine; Chianti's image was low, and its market was
depressed. Some producers felt they could make a
better wine (and receive a higher price for it) by using
unconventional grape varieties or blends, and winemaking methods borrowed from places such as
Bordeaux, that produce high quality wines. These new
wines didn't qualify as DOC Chianti, and so they were
labelled as *vino da tavola di Toscana*. The most
common blends were Sangiovese and Cabernet
Sauvignon, or wines that were entirely Cabernet or
entirely Sangiovese.

The trend of Super-Tuscan wine production spread
beyond the borders of Chianti Classico to every corner
of Tuscany, as winemakers sought to show off their
talent and make profitable wines. (Actually, the first
Super-Tuscan wine didn't come from the Chianti zone
but from Bolgheri, near the Tuscan coast, but the
movement gained its impetus in Chianti.) It even
spread to other parts of Italy, where today you can

find a few Super-Veneto wines, for example, or
Super-Piedmonteses — although they're never really
called that.

No official or even complete listing of all Super-Tuscan
wines exists. We wanted to be the first to do it, but the
task is overwhelming. Besides, a lot of confusion
exists over what is and isn't a Super-Tuscan wine
today, because some of the original Super-Tuscan
wines, such as Sassicaia (sas-ee-*kye*-ah), are now DOC
wines. That's part of the difficulty in having an unofficial category. The best we can do is to list here some of
our favorite Super-Tuscan wines (some of which are
DOC wines), in alphabetical order, along with their
grape/s and producer (when we list Cabernet, we refer
to Cabernet Sauvignon):

Cepparello, Sangiovese (Isole e Olena)

Grattamacco, Sangiovese, Malvasia Nera, Cabernet
(Grattamacco)

Masseto, Merlot (Tenuta dell'Ornellaia)

Ornellaia, mainly Cabernet Sauvignon; some Merlot,
Cabernet Franc (Tenuta dell'Ornellaia)

Percarlo, Sangiovese (San Giusto a Rentennano)

Le Pergole Torte, Sangiovese (Montevertine)

Prunaio, mainly Sangiovese (Viticcio)

Sammarco, ⅚ Cabernet; ⅙ Sangiovese (Castello di
Rampolla)

Sassicaia, 75-25 percent Cabernet Sauvignon-Cabernet
Franc (Tenuta San Guido)

I Sodi di San Niccolò, mostly Sangiovese; some
Malvasia Nera (Castellare di Castellina)

Solaia, 80-20 percent Cabernet -Sangiovese (Antinori)

Tignanello, 80-20 percent Sangiovese-Cabernet
(Antinori)

Chapter 4
The Wines of Southern Italy

. . . .

In This Chapter

► Campania's untapped potential

► Sturdy reds from Puglia

► Basilicata's Aglianico del Vulture

► The rustic wines of Calabria

. . . .

Southern Italy has a proud wine history. The area has produced wine for over 4,000 years; in 2,000 B.C., when Phoenician traders arrived in what is today the region of Apulia, a local wine industry was already thriving! The Greeks later dubbed Southern Italy, "The Land of Wine."

Within the last decade this area has begun a long-awaited wine renaissance, producing fine wines from quality-conscious producers.

Campania: Revival Begins

Campania sits along Italy's western coast, on the Tyrrhenian Sea (see Figure 1-1). More than half of Campania's terrain consists of hillsides. The climate is mainly hot and dry near the sea, but can be cool and rainy, especially in the autumn, in the inland Apennines.

Just ten short years ago, more than half of the region's DOC wine came from *one* producer! That producer, Mastroberardino, is still the leader in DOC wine production, but today several others have finally joined the ranks of quality-conscious firms willing to tap Campania's tremendous potential. One of their key assets is a red grape variety, Aglianico (ah-l'yee-*ah*-nee-co), which has proven to be one of the great, noble grapes of Italy; also, two white varieties, Fiano and Greco di Tufo, make some of the very best, long-lived white wines in the country. It's safe to say that in a few years, Campania will be regarded as one of Italy's "hot" wine regions.

The best of Campania's DOC wines can be grouped geographically into three areas:

- ✔ The Irpinia hills of Avellino, in central Campania
- ✔ The coastal hills and islands around Naples
- ✔ The northern hills of the region

The wines of Avellino

Campania's three greatest wines come from the Irpinia hills around the city of Avellino, the capital of the Avellino province: the red Taurasi, and two DOC whites, Fiano di Avellino and Greco di Tufo.

Until recently, the only winery that mattered in Avellino was Mastroberardino, owned by a family that has produced wine for about 300 years. Since the 1970s, Antonio Mastroberardino has been responsible for dramatic improvements not only in the wines of Avellino, but also in the wines of the coastal hills area.

But in the past decade, Feudi di San Gregorio, another very good, but smaller, producer, whose consulting enologist is the renowned Riccardo Cotarella, began producing wines that challenged Mastroberardino's monopoly.

Taurasi

Mastroberardino's 1968 Taurasi Riserva won so much acclaim worldwide that it brought this massive red wine — and its noble grape variety, Aglianico — attention it had never before received. Taurasi (touw-*rah*-see) is a wine that demands aging, not unlike the other great Italian reds — Barolo, Barbaresco, and Brunello. In good vintages, this complex, powerful, and tannic wine is at its best after 15 to 20 years.

Taurasi's vineyard area is the hills around the community of Taurasi and 16 others, northeast of Avellino. The wine must be at least 85 percent Aglianico, with up to 15 percent other red varieties, but in practice, most of the better Taurasi wines are 100 percent Aglianico. Taurasi must age for at least three years before being released, at least one of which is in wood; Taurasi Riservas must age for at least four years (including at least 18 months in wood). Taurasi wines retail in the $32 to $40 price range. Mastroberardino's finest Taurasi is the single-vineyard "Radici"; other good Taurasi wines are made by Feudi di San Gregorio and Terredora.

Fiano di Avellino

At its best, Fiano di Avellino is Southern Italy's top dry white wine — and one of the best in the entire country. It's a delicately-flavored wine with aromas of pear and toasted hazelnuts, which become more pronounced with age. Unlike most dry white wines, Fiano di Avellino is best with at least five or six years of aging, and will be fine for up to 15, in good vintages.

The DOC zone for this wine is the hills around Avellino and 25 other communities, a few of which are in the Taurasi DOCG zone; the best Fiano vineyards are in the hills around Lapio. Fiano di Avellino must have at least 85 percent Fiano grapes, with the balance Greco and/or Coda di Volpe and/or Trebbiano Toscano. Fiano di Avellino wines retail for about $18 to $24. Wines to look for include Terredora's single-vineyard Terre di Dora, Mastroberardino's single-vineyard Vignadora or Radici, and Feudi di San Gregorio's Pietracalda.

Greco di Tufo

The name Greco di Tufo (*greh*-co-dee-*too*-foh) applies to both a white grape variety and a DOC wine. The Greeks introduced the Greco variety to Italy over 2,000 years ago. It flourishes in many parts of Italy, but the particular clone (called Greco di Tufo) that grows around the hillside village of Tufo and seven other communities directly north of Avellino is undoubtedly the best. "Tufa" or "tufo" is a type of calcareous rock deposited by springs or lakes; the tufaceous and volcanic soil of the Tufo area makes an auspicious environment for this grape.

Greco di Tufo is similar to Fiano di Avellino; the differences are that Greco di Tufo wines are more intensely fruity and crisper; Fiano di Avellino wines are more subtle and a bit softer. Greco di Tufo also ages well, but not quite so long as Fiano; Greco di Tufo is usually ready to drink after three or four years, but can age for at least 10 to 12 years. Greco di Tufo wines must derive at least 85 percent from Greco, with the balance Coda di Volpe. Look for the Greco di Tufo wines of Feudi di San Gregorio, Mastroberardino — especially the single-vineyard Vignadangelo — and Terredora. Greco di Tufo retails for about $17 to $23.

Wines of the coastal hills and islands around Naples

The coastal hills and islands around Naples have seven DOC wines. Three of them, Ischia, Capri, and Vesuvio, are longstanding. **Ischia** (*ees*-key-ah) actually became Italy's second DOC wine, in 1966. And that's not the only history this wine has going for it: The Greeks planted grapes on this island in 770 B.C. Not much wine is made today, but white wines dominate production, with D'Ambra Vini d'Ischia making the island's best. Ischia Bianco is mainly Forastera, with Biancolella and other white grapes; the same varieties also make a Bianco *spumante,* and each of these two grapes makes a varietal wine. Ischia Rosso is a dry red mainly from Guarnaccia (in the Grenache family) and Piedirosso (known locally as Pér'e Palummo); Piedirosso also makes a varietal wine and a *passito*.

Capri (*cah*-pree), the island at the end of the Sorrento Peninsula, is such a wealthy tourist mecca that vineyards or winemaking don't get much attention. Capri's extremely limited vineyards are on terraced slopes with calcareous soil, and overlook the sea. Capri has two wines: Capri Bianco (mainly Falanghina and Greco, with up to 20 percent Biancolella); and Capri Rosso (mainly Piedirosso).

Lacryma Christi del Vesuvio (*lah*-cree-mah-*chree*-sti-de-veh-*soo*-vee-oh), also called Vesuvio, comes from vineyards on the slopes of Mount Vesuvius, east of Naples, overlooking the Bay of Naples. The area has great volcanic soil, but had very little quality wine until Mastroberardino came along. Vesuvio's wines can be white, red, or rosé. The basic wines, with less than 12 percent alcohol, carry the simpler Vesuvio DOC, while

the white, red, or rosé wines from riper grapes are
Lacryma Christi ("tears of Christ") del Vesuvio. The
Bianco is mainly Verdeca and Coda di Volpe, with up to
20 percent Greco and/or Falanghina; the Rosso and
Rosato are mainly Piedirosso and Sciascinoso, with up
to 20 percent Aglianico. All three Lacryma Christi wines
can also be *spumante*.

Since 1990, four new DOC wine areas have joined these
three:

- **Campi Flegrei** (*cahm-pee-fleh-*grae): Of
  Campania's newer DOC zones, this area has the
  most promise. Campi Flegrei Bianco is a dry white
  made mainly from Falanghina, Biancolella, and
  Coda di Volpe varieties; Campi Flegrei Falanghina
  is a dry white varietal — or a *spumante* — derived
  at least 90 percent from that variety. Campi Flegrei
  Rosso is a dry red (or *novello* style) mainly from
  Piedirosso, Aglianico, and Sciascinoso grapes.
  Campi Flegrei Piedirosso — dry or *passito* — must
  contain at least 90 percent of this variety.

- **Costa d'Amalfi** (*cohs-*tah-dah-*mahl-*fee): The Costa
  d'Amalfi DOC features Bianco, Rosso, and Rosato
  wines. The Bianco is at least 60 percent
  Falanghina and Biancolella; the Rosso and Rosato
  are at least 60 percent Piedirosso and Sciascinoso.

- **Penisola Sorrentina** (peh-*nee-*so-lahf-sor-ren-*tee-*
  nah): The Sorrento Peninsula zone is known for its
  fizzy red wines, but has lost many of its vineyards
  due to Naples' expansion. Penisola Sorrentina
  Bianco is mainly Falanghina, Biancolella, and/or
  Greco; the Rosso and Rosso *frizzante naturale* are
  mainly Piedirosso, Sciascinoso, and/or Aglianico.

- **Asprinio di Aversa** (ahs-*pree*-nee-oh-dee-ah-*vehr*-sa): This wine zone makes a dry white wine from at least 85 percent Asprinio grapes; in its more popular form, Asprinio di Aversa is a dry *spumante,* from 100 percent Asprinio. Aversa has been a declining wine area that hopes the blessing of DOC status can revive it.

Campania's northern hills

Northern Campania is dominated by the Apennine Mountains and their foothills; it includes some historic wine districts, such as Falerno del Massico, on the coastline, which dates back to Roman times, and quite a few new, developing wine areas. The climate varies considerably. The coastal area of Falerno is warm, and produces plump wines redolent of fruit; wine zones further inland have a cooler Apennine-influenced climate, and more austere wines. Northern Campania now has seven DOC wines:

- **Falerno del Massico** (fah-*ler*-no-del-*mah*-see-co): Today, three styles of Falerno del Massico exist: a Bianco (most likely made from a different variety than it was 2,000 years ago), a Rosso, and a Primitivo. Villa Matilde and Fontana Galardi are two leading wineries.

- **Gallucio** (gahl-*loo*-cho): Gallucio's vineyards occupy the hills around an extinct volcano, where the soil is rich in minerals. The wines are similar to Falerno's, but tend to be a bit lighter and have more aromatic finesse.

✔ **Solopaca** (so-lo-*pah*-cah): This wine zone in north-central Campania is in a valley between two mountain ranges, and is named for the village of Solopaca. Six types of wine carry the Solopaca DOC: a Rosso, Rosato, Bianco, two varietal wines, and a *spumante*.

✔ **Taburno** (tah-*bur*-no): Taburno has a varietal Aglianico (Rosso or Rosato), Falanghina, Greco, and Coda di Volpe (all whites), and Piedirosso.

✔ **Sant'Agata dei Goti** (sahnt-*ahg*-ah-tah-dae-*go*-tee): A Bianco, Rosso, *novello*, and Rosato — all from the same varieties (no, we didn't make a mistake!). Those varieties are Aglianico and Piedirosso, both reds (other non-aromatic red varieties may be added); the Bianco is made using only the color-less juice of the grapes, and not their red skins.

✔ **Guardiolo** (gwar-dee-*oh*-lo): Guardiolo Bianco is a dry white made mainly from Malvasia Bianca di Candia and Falanghina; a Rosso and Rosato are mainly Sangiovese. Guardiolo Aglianico is a dry red with at least 90 percent of that variety, and Guardiolo Falanghina is a dry white 90 percent varietal, with Malvasia Bianca and/or other white grapes; a *spumante* is a dry sparkling wine made from the same varieties as the Falanghina.

✔ **Sannio** (*sahn*-nee-oh): This is a new, general wine zone covering the entire Benevento province, as a catch-all designation for wines outside the province's other DOC zones.

Campania wines worth buying

 A few of our recommended wine producers in Campania are listed alphabetically:

Antonio Caggiano

La Caprense

Marisa Cuomo

De Concilus

Feudi di San Gregorio

Luigi Maffini

Mastroberardino

S. Molettieri

Montevetrano

Ocone

Terredora

Villa Matilde

Villa San Michele

Apulia: Italy's Wine Barrel

Apulia, or Puglia (*poo*-l'yah), as the Italians call it, is truly Italy's wine lake, producing between 100 and 130 million cases of wine annually. About 80 percent of Puglia's wine is red, but less than 4 percent of it is DOC; most of it is unremarkable wine made by large-volume cooperatives that's shipped north in bulk to improve the less robust red wines of cooler climes.

Puglia's three major grape varieties are Negroamaro, Primitivo, and Malvasia Nera — all red grapes. These grapes grow mainly on the Salento Peninsula — the spike of Italy's boot — and most of the wines of that area are made from one, or a blend, of them. Negroamaro and Primitivo, in fact, are Italy's fourth and sixth most-planted red grape varieties — even though they grow mainly just in Puglia.

Puglia's most notable DOC wines are the following regions:

- ✔ The Salento Peninsula, the most important area for quality
- ✔ The "Trulli" district, north of the Salento peninsula
- ✔ Central Apulia, including Castel del Monte, a quality zone

The Salento Peninsula

The Salento Peninsula is Puglia's major wine district and its 11 DOC wines include the renowned Salice Salentino and Primitivo di Manduria. Most of its wines are dark and robust, with ripe flavors and rather high alcohol content. They're made mainly from Negroamaro and/or Primitivo, with Malvasia Nera the third most important grape. (But Aglianico, Campania's noble red grape — and in our opinion the best red variety in Southern Italy — is an emerging presence in the peninsula, either for varietal or, more commonly, blended red wines.)

Salice Salentino

Salice Salentino (*sah*-lee-chae-sah-len-*tee*-no) is Puglia's wine ambassador: It's the one Apulian wine that many winedrinkers abroad have tasted, or at least heard of. It's a dark, robust wine of the South, with all the warm, ripe, even slightly baked, flavors of sun-drenched grapes. It's made mainly from Negroamaro, with up to 20 percent Malvasia Nera.

The late Cosimo Taurino, whose wines have had great success on the U.S. market (and whose son, Francesco, continues his work), favored a lusty style for this wine. He made his Salice Salentino — and his two other, even classier Negroamaro wines, Notapanaro and Patriglione — from extra-ripe grapes, to achieve this style. Basic Salice Salentino retails for $10 to $11, but special, single-vineyard versions run anywhere from $12 to $30, and Graticciaia costs about $35.

Primitivo di Manduria

Primitivo di Manduria (pre-meh-*tee*-vo-dee-mahn-*doo*-ree-ah) is both the name of a DOC wine and the name of a grape. Of the various types of Primitivo grapes, this is the one thought to be genetically the same as Zinfandel. Surely, Primitivo di Manduria wines share certain characteristics with Zinfandel: They're dark in color (although some red American Zins are made in a lighter style), they're usually high in alcohol, and they're rich and opulently fruity. If anything, Primitivo seems to make wines that are bigger in every way than most Zinfandels, starting with their deep purple color (which is partly due to the fact that the juice of the grapes is dark, rather than colorless).

Primitivo di Manduria wine always comes 100 percent from that grape. (What other variety could compete with it?) It's rich, ripe, and explosively fruity; its *minimum* alcohol content is 14 percent but usually higher. Although it can age for a few years, it's best young.

The Perucci brothers — who make wine under the Pervini (an acronym for "Perucci Vini"), Felline, and Sinfarosa brands—are greatly responsible for the improvement of wines in this DOC zone. Formerly, the

wines were rough and rustic — like some rowdy rela-
tion you enjoy but try to avoid introducing to polite
company. But lately, Primitivo di Manduria wines have
taken on an elegance — relatively speaking, since high-
alcohol reds trade on power rather than subtlety or
finesse — that they didn't previously have. You can
find Primitivo di Manduria retailing for $9 to $12 —
although Sinfarosa makes one called "Zinfandel," which
sells for $20. Primitivo di Manduria also comes in three
dessert styles: *dolce naturale* (minimum alcohol, 16 percent); *liquoroso dolce naturale* (minimum alcohol,
17.5 percent); and *liquoroso secco* (minimum alcohol,
18 percent). With two glasses of these wines, you'll eat
the whole cake.

Other Salento Peninsula wines

Three other Salento Peninsula DOC wines of note are:

- **Brindisi** (*breen*-deh-see): Named after the coastal
  town of Brindisi, this is a dry, rich red wine (or a
  rosé) that's mainly Negroamaro, with up to 30 percent Montepulciano and/or Malvasia Nera and/or
  Susumaniello (a Croatian variety), and
  Sangiovese. Cosimo Taurino's greatest wine,
  Patriglione, mainly Negroamaro, is Brindisi's finest
  wine; Agricole Vallone also makes good Brindisi
  wines.

- **Copertino** (co-per-*tee*-no): These dry red and rosé
  wines are mainly Negroamaro, with up to 30 percent Malvasia Nera and/or Montepulciano, plus up
  to 15 percent Sangiovese. The great enologist of
  the Salento Peninsula, Severino Garofano, con-
  sults at wineries in Copertino, and so quality is
  high here.

✔ **Alezio** (ah-*leh*-zee-oh): The dry Alezio Rosso (or Rosato) is mainly Negroamaro, with Malvasia Nera, Sangiovese, or Montepulciano, together or singly. This small zone is east of coastal Gallipoli. The leading winery is Calò's Rosa del Golfo, which makes one of Italy's best dry rosés, from Negroamaro and Malvasia Nera.

The "Trulli" district

The Trulli district, south of the city of Bari, is an area of valleys and gorges carved by the Itria River. Unique to this area are the unusual, conical-roofed, triangular-shaped stone dwellings, called *trulli,* built to counteract the sometimes harsh heat of the area. Ironically, considering the heat, two of the four DOC wines of the district are white; they're grown in a belt where the clashing currents of the Adriatic and Ionian Seas bring cool breezes and summer rain.

Puglia's most renowned white wine is **Locorotondo** (lo-co-ro-*tohn*-doh). It's a dry white made mainly from Verdeca with 35 to 50 percent Bianco di Alessano, and Fiano and/or Bombino Bianco and/or Malvasia Toscana optional. A *spumante* style also exists. **Martina Franca** (or Martina) is the other white DOC wine of the Trulli district. It's very similar to Locorotondo, with exactly the same grape varieties. Martina Franca, the community which is the center of this wine zone, is a dramatic, *trulli* hill town, five miles south of Locorotondo.

Vineyards around the ancient town of **Ostuni** (oh-*stew*-nee), northwest of the coastal city of Brindisi, make Ostuni Ottavianello — a dry, light-bodied, cherry-red wine made from Ottavianello (France's Cinsault variety) and Ostuni Bianco, a dry white mainly from the local Impigno and Francavilla.

Castel del Monte

Castel del Monte is the most important DOC wine in the Bari province of Central Puglia.

In the 13th century, the Norman Emperor Friedrich II, then ruler of this region, built a magnificent, octagon-shaped castle on a high plateau (known as the Murge) near the community of Andria, west of the city of Bari. The castle, known as Castel del Monte, remains one of the great sights of Puglia, and gives the name to this rather large wine zone.

Castel del Monte's best producer is Rivera, a longstanding leader here, whose Rosso Riserva "Il Falcone" is internationally renowned. Recently, the area has attracted outside investment, such as Tuscany's Antinori firm, which, under the name Vigneti del Sud, purchased 250 acres of land here (plus 1,250 acres in the Salento peninsula).

Castel del Monte can be a blended Rosso, Rosato or Bianco wine or one of seven varietal wines. The Rosso is a dry red mainly from Uva di Troia and/or Aglianico and/or Montepulciano, with up to 35 percent other red varieties. The dry Rosato derives from Bombino Nera and/or Aglianico and/or Uva di Troia, and up to 35 percent other red varieties. The Bianco is a dry white mainly from Pampanuto (an indigenous variety) and/or Chardonnay and/or Bombino Bianco, with up to 35 percent other white varieties.

Recommended Puglia producers

Almost all of Puglia's best wines are red, and a large majority of them come from the Salento Peninsula and are based on Negroamaro, Puglia's leading variety — except when they're Primitivo wines. Our recommended wine producers in Puglia are listed alphabetically:

Botromagno	Masseria Pepe
Candido	Rivera
Cantina del Locorotondo	Sinfarosa
D'Alfonso del Sordo	Cosimo Taurino
Felline	Agricole Vallone
Lomazzi & Sarli	Valle dell'Asso
Nugnes	Conti Zecca

Mountainous Basilicata

If it weren't for Aglianico del Vulture, we could have skipped right over Basilicata. But Aglianico del Vulture is a serious wine worth trying. It's mainly a dry, powerful red — but *amabile* and sweet *spumante* versions are also made, although rarely exported.

The wine derives entirely from the austere, tannic Aglianico variety, and like all Aglianico-based wines, it requires aging; when its black-red color starts to turn to ruby, and its blackberry aromas begin to evolve, usually after about five years, you can begin to enjoy the wine.

Basic Aglianico del Vulture ages a minimum of one year at the winery, but wines labeled *vecchio* (old) age for at least three years, and those labeled *Riserva* age for at least five years before release. Aglianico del Vulture wines, especially the *vecchio* and *Riservas*, improve for ten years or more, especially in good vintages. Most Aglianico del Vulture wines retail for $16 to $20.

The leading producers of Aglianico del Vulture are: Basilium, D'Angelo, Armando Martino, Paternoster, and Francesco Sessa.

Rugged Calabria

Another primarily mountainous region, Calabria is the "ball" and "toe" of Italy's boot, and the southernmost region of the Italian mainland.

Calabria is a poor region, and wine is a minor product, less important in the region's economy than olive oil, produce, and grains. The climate along both coastlines is hot and dry, but winters are cold and harsh in the interior mountains, especially in northern Calabria. Most of the region's wines come from the central part of both the eastern and western coasts.

Only 4 percent of Calabria's wine has DOC status. In fact, only a few independent producers and cooperatives even bottle their wine; much of Calabria's sturdy, high-alcohol wine is sold in bulk to wineries in Northern Italy and nearby countries.

Although 12 DOC wine zones now exist in the region, only one, Cirò, on the east-central coast, has gained any recognition outside of Calabria; most of the other wines are consumed locally.

Ciró comes in red, white, and rosé styles, but the red is the area's best wine. Cirò Rosso and Rosato are dry wines from at least 95 percent Gaglioppo, with Trebbiano and/or Greco Bianco optional. A good Cirò Rosso is full-bodied, powerful, tannic, fruity, and soft; it's at its best when it's consumed within three or four years of the vintage. Cirò Bianco is a dry white from at least 90 percent Greco Bianco, with Trebbiano optional. The *classico* designation is for Cirò Rosso only.

To say that Cirò is spearheading a Calabrian wine resurgence would be overstating the case. Most of Cirò is still bound to the past; many common technological winemaking practices, such as temperature-controlled fermentation, have barely arrived in Calabria. But two Cirò wineries — Librandi and Fattoria San Francesco — have employed enologists and are taking the necessary steps to make quality wine. The basic Cirò Rosso from these wineries retails for a mere $10 to $11, and their *riservas* are $15 to $16.

We can only recommend five producers of Calabrian wines, but this is partially because much of Calabria's limited production of bottled wines never leaves the region. The three private wineries and the two cooperatives that we *do* recommend, listed alphabetically, are the progressive, quality leaders in the region today: Cantine Lamezia Lento and Caparra & Siciliani (both co-ops); Fattoria San Francesco, Librandi, and Odoardi.

With more than 1,400 titles to choose from, we've got a Dummies book for wherever you are in life!

Business/Personal Finance & Investment

High-Powered Investing All-in-One For Dummies	9780470186268	$29.99
Investing For Dummies, 5th Edition	9780470289655	$21.99
Living Well in a Down Economy For Dummies	9780470401170	$14.99
Managing Your Money All-in-One For Dummies	9780470345467	$29.99
Personal Finance Workbook For Dummies	9780470099339	$19.99
Taxes 2009 For Dummies (January 2009)	9780470249512	$17.99

Crafts & Hobbies

California Wine For Dummies (May 2009)	9780470376072	$16.99
Canning & Preserving For Dummies	9780764524714	$16.99
Jewelry & Beading Designs For Dummies	9780470291122	$19.99
Knitting For Dummies, 2nd Edition	9780470287477	$21.99
Quilting For Dummies, 2nd Edition	9780764597992	$21.99
Watercolor Painting For Dummies	9780470182314	$24.99

Fitness & Diet

Dieting For Dummies, 2nd Edition	9780764541490	$21.99
Low-Calorie Dieting For Dummies	9780764599057	$21.99
Nutrition For Dummies, 4th Edition	9780471798682	$21.99
Exercise Balls For Dummies	9780764556234	$21.99
Fitness For Dummies, 3rd Edition	9780764578519	$21.99
Stretching For Dummies	9780470067413	$16.99